John MacArthur
and the
Christian Evolution

Neal Wooten

ISBN 978-1-61225-003-8

Published by Mirror Publishing
Milwaukee, WI 53214
www.pagesofwonder.com

Printed in the USA

Table of Contents

John Fullerton MacArthur, Jr. (born June 19, 1939) is a United States evangelical writer and minister, noted for his radio program entitled Grace to You. MacArthur is a fifth-generation pastor, a popular author and conference speaker and has served as the pastor-teacher of Grace Community Church in Sun Valley, California since 1969, and as the President of The Master's College (and the related The Master's Seminary) in Santa Clarita, California.

Theologically, MacArthur is a dispensationalist and Calvinist, and a strong proponent of expository preaching. He has been acknowledged by Christianity Today as one of the most influential preachers of his time, and is a frequent guest on Larry King Live as representative of an evangelical Christian perspective

http://en.wikipedia.org

John MacArthur, the gifted and charming pastor of Grace Community Church in Panorama City, California, has been the center of controversy for many years. He appears to be one of those rare individuals whose presence leaves a wake of confusion and contention. For many, he is a champion of the faith whose voice is correcting many of the ills of Christianity. For others, his teachings border on heresy. He is seen by these as a threat to the Christian faith.

Much has already been written concerning John MacArthur. What good could another article about him accomplish? Why should the VISITOR get involved in the fray? If John MacArthur is being unjustly criticized, he should be defended. If, on the other hand, John MacArthur is doing damage to the body of Christ, he should be exposed. In either case, the influence of John MacArthur and its subsequent confusion have reached into the ranks of fundamental Christianity. Silence is not an option.

www.gnbcbible.com

Introduction

Back in the mid 90's, I was reunited with an old friend whom I had always really liked. But, as usually happens with old friends, we each had gotten busy with our own lives and lost touch.

As we reminisced about the old days and caught up on the new, I was happy to hear that he and his wife, another old friend, were firmly rooted in their church. He spoke about God and Jesus in an easy manner that was a comfort to hear.

Somehow, during the course of the conversation, we got onto a different subject. We talked about how when we visit large grocery stores, or other public places, some people approach asking for money for food. When he asked me how I handled that, I was honest.

"I never give it to them," I said. "I believe that most of them, if not all, want it for drugs and I don't want to contribute to that. How do you handle it?" I asked.

He simply replied, "I always give it to them if I have it."

"Really?" I was shocked wondering how someone could be so gullible in this day and age. "Why?"

His words were soft and earnest. "Like you said, there could be a small percentage that really need it. There's no way to tell. I would not feel comfortable thinking I could have refused to help a needy person. If they were lying about what they wanted the money for, that's between them and God."

I was suddenly ashamed of my answer. His message

was so simple. We cannot tell what is in another person's heart, but it should never affect what is in our own. His message was so encouraging and uplifting, I tried to live up to it as well.

About ten years later, I came into contact again with that same great, old friend. As we talked, we relived part of that old conversation from a decade earlier. I was glad to tell him how he changed my life and that something he had said back then still resonated with me today. He was curious as to what it was so I reminded him of what he had said about people asking for money.

"Oh," he laughed. "No, I don't think that way now."

If you had kicked me in the stomach, it would have not felt worse than those words.

As our conversation instinctively led to Christianity and the Bible, I was shocked at his current views. They seemed so foreign to me, dark even. Then he started quoting John MacArthur and I understood.

I had only recently become aware of MacArthur's teachings about a year earlier while posting on a public on line Christian message board. Almost all the people posting messages were very well read, informative, caring, and respectful

But I was shocked when two people kept writing what I considered to be things very contrary to Christianity. I soon learned from their own words that they were followers of MacArthur.

This led me to find out more about John MacArthur and

7

what he taught. And once I started reading his writings, I began to understand the posters' reactionary stance.

Every follower of MacArthur I have met since discusses the Bible and Christianity in the same abrupt manner. If offered a view different from their own, it seems to be taken personally and they feel the need to not only correct you, but do it in an offensive manner.

This was also the same kind of responses that any mere questioning of the ideas posted by the MacArthurian Christians brought to the message board. It didn't matter what the subject was about: the Elect, the Tribulation, the Trinity, creation, etc., if your idea didn't match their idea, you were quickly attacked and labeled a fool or hypocrite or worse.

I will admit that in all my years, this was the first time I had ever witnessed professed Christians attacking other Christians over trivial matters.

I tried to point out that the arguments themselves were moot. The Bible never says that we must fully comprehend every single aspect of God and how He works. A lot of that is beyond our comprehension.

In short, I tried to remind them that the Bible says that God rewards obedience, and never does it say that intelligence or even education is rewarded.

Proverbs 3:5-6
5 Trust in the LORD with all your heart and lean not on your own understanding; 6 in all your ways acknowledge him, and he will make your paths straight. (NIV)

Of course that too brought about the same crude responses full of immature attacks.

It was for this reason that I began to study the teachings of John MacArthur and the more I studied, the more I was surprised.

I do not have a ministry nor do I follow any ministry so I have no hidden agenda. I am not trying to prove that I am right and MacArthur is wrong. I am not trying to claim that he is the correction for Christianity's ills, or if his teachings border upon heresy. I have nothing to gain or lose either way. I would just like to present some comparisons to the teachings of John MacArthur in reference to the Bible messages they correlate to.

Any conclusions I leave up to you.

MacArthurian Christians would probably interject here and ask how many books on the subject I've written, how many Bibles I've written, how many years of seminary I've had, and how many degrees in seminary I have. They have, in fact, asked me that many times.

I can honestly and humbly answer – none, the same number as most Christians and the same number Jesus had.

But herein you'll discover a fundamental different in me and them. I believe the teachings of Jesus Christ are simple and easy to understand. They seem to believe that you need an expert to explain the words of Jesus.

And MacArthur does that in great detail in his lectures, sermons, articles, and interviews. But to me, his explanations seem many times to be 180 degrees different than what the

9

Bible teaches.

There are many, many examples to choose from but I will concentrate on only a few.

For the purpose of this book The words of MacArthur will appear indented on each side, in Arial Bold Italics.

Passages from the Bible will appear like this in Times New Roman in white with black background.

Bible passages are taken from either the New International Version or the King James Bible.

Exerts from MacArthur are taken directly from books, articles, or transcripts of sermons and interviews and most can be found on his website – www.gty.org – and are the property of John MacArthur and/or the Grace to You ministries.

Chapter One: Evolution

Evo-lu-tion
A process of change in a certain direction.
(Merriam-Webster online dictionary)

I know it seems odd to combine the words "Christian" and "evolution," but as you can see by Webster's definition, evolution is simply change is a certain direction. And that's what I've seen taking place with Christianity, especially in the United States and especially in the last three decades.

I think it would be fair to say that it began under the Reagan Administration, or at least began to accelerate. I do not want to make this book about politics, but I would be remiss to not mention the impact that politics has played on Christian beliefs.

The successful marriage of the Republican Party and the Christian Right began a transformation of mainstream Christianity. Certain policies of the GOP obviously had more appeal to Christians. For example, it makes sense that a Christian would not support abortion or gay marriage.

This union with the GOP, however, seemed to shift more and more views of most Christians further to the right than they had been before. It was almost as if the teachings of Jesus were being adapted to better fit into that mold.

Then came the events of 9/11. Ever since that date, no longer did we as Americans ever want to feel like we belonged to the weaker religion. And passive characteristics like love, compassion, and forgiveness seem much weaker than hatred, aggression, and tyranny.

They are not weaker traits, but they can seem so.

There have been Calvinists and dispensationalists around for a long time, maintaining a small but dedicated presence on the outskirts of Christianity. But those ideas have gained new footholds in the last few decades. Factor in the political influence and then the dangers from terrorists, and now these ideas which had for a long time been characterized as extreme, now suddenly have more appeal to mainstream Christians.

John MacArthur's teachings hit right at the core of a lot of these changes and his influence appears to be growing beyond his non-denominational Grace Community fellowship and is striking cords with more and more Christians from more traditional, denominational sects.

To me, being a Christian has always been about discipline and personal sacrifice, which makes it very hard. I believe that salvation is a combination of works and deeds. If a person has faith, but continually breaks the Commandments or instructions from Jesus with no remorse, I can't see them being on the narrow road that leads to life that only a few find.

Yes, Jesus died for our sins, but I don't believe that means we now live in a state of perpetual forgiveness. I believe it means that now we can always atone for our sins as long as we truly seek forgiveness in our hearts.

Ever since the original sin, humans are filled with human desires such as greed, judgment, aggression, etc. I believe as a Christian, one should strive to rise above those things.

But what I get from reading the teachings of John MacArthur is the idea that it's ok to be these things, at least some of them. In fact, from what I read, he seems to try to explain that Christians are supposed to judge, be aggressive, and have other traits that I see in direct conflict with the words of Jesus.

I can see how that can be appealing to people. If you tell them that it's ok to act on your human nature and that this is what Christians are supposed to do, and that you were chosen to be one of the saved anyway, well, that can be a very appealing message to all of us.

Testament
a covenant between God and the human race.
Merriam-Webster online dictionary.

Covenant
a usually formal, solemn, and binding agreement.
Merriam-Webster online dictionary.

In a discussion with several MacArthurian Christians about Jesus promoting compassion and love, a subject they seem to want to argue until the end, one of them offered this scripture as proof of a Christian's duty to be the tough aggressor.

> Exodus 22:2
> If a thief is caught breaking in and is struck so that he dies, the defender is not guilty of bloodshed;
> (NIV)

"Exodus?" I asked. "That's the Old Testament."

In unison they began to inform me that the Old Testament is still to be applied today.

I argued that the moral lessons can be applied, but not the old criminal and civil laws. I pointed out that this was an old law of a certain area but to no avail. I also pointed out the very next verses in hopes that it would show how ridiculous their claim to be.

> Exodus 22:3-4
> 3 but if it happens after sunrise, he is guilty of bloodshed. 4 A thief must certainly make restitution, but if he has nothing, he must be sold to pay for his theft.
> (NIV)

I asked them if they would also agree that if it happened in the daytime, they would be guilty of murder and if they truly believed that a person today could still be sold into slavery.

I got no response.

This seems to be a common practice among MacArthurian Christians - take pieces of scripture to back up your views and discard the rest.

When I think back to my first 30 years of attending different churches, as a child or an adult well into the late 90's, there seemed to be one consistent view of the two Testaments of the Bible. The Old Testament, or old covenant, was exactly that; it was the old agreement between God and the Hebrews.

The New Testament was also what the name implied, the new agreement between God and Christians set forth to coincide with the arrival of the Christ.

It has always been said that the Old Testament is an important and necessary study guide to understand the beginning, the fall of man, the flood, God's wrath, and judgment in general.

But for the MacArthurian Christian, it seems to be more than that. Because the Old Testament is filled with war, violence, judgment and punishment, it has become a veritable fountain of resources to thwart the "gentle" teachings of Jesus in the New Testament.

John MacArthur appears to be a staunch believer in using The Old Testament, not just for study purposes, but for application as well.

In his article, "Pleasing One Another for the Sake of Christ," he writes:

> *"A. The Value of Scripture*
> *In his justification for using the Old Testament in verse 3, Paul affirms the value of Scripture in general. The phrase "whatever things were written in earlier times" refers to the Old Testament. Second Peter 1:21 says, "Holy men of God spoke as they were moved by the Holy Spirit." That verse also refers to the Old Testament. The phrase "was written for our learning" tells us that the Old Testament is not a dead book. First Corinthians 10:6, 11 tell us it provides us with examples. Paul said to Timothy, "All Scripture is given by inspiration of God, and is profitable for doctrine, for reproof, for correction, for instruction in righteousness, that the man of God may be perfect, thoroughly furnished unto all good works" (2 Tim. 3:16 17)."*

This is one of many references made by John MacArthur to justify applying the Old Testament to Christianity today. But nowhere in his teachings have I found what parts of the Old Testament are to be followed, or even a formula for determining how to decide which parts are to be followed.

I have gotten this passage, 2 Timothy 3:16-17, many times from MacArthurian Christians to try to prove that the Bible instructs us to still follow the Old Testament.

2 Timothy 3:16-17
16All Scripture is God-breathed and is useful for teaching, rebuking, correcting and training in righteousness, 17so that the man of God may be thoroughly equipped for every good work.
(NIV)

But notice that it says that all scripture is useful for several different things: teaching, rebuking, correcting, and training. Everyone knows that the Old Testament is great for teaching, teaching about the creation, the flood, etc. But this does not even imply that one should follow all the rules of the Old Testament. It just doesn't say it.

And here is an undisputable fact: for all the talk of applying "all scripture," even MacArthur and MacArthurian Christians could only be applying parts of the Old Testament since today's criminal laws would not permit the practice of a lot of thing mentioned in the Old Testament.

Here are just a few:

Deuteronomy 17:12)
12 The man who shows contempt for the judge or for the priest who stands ministering there to the LORD your God must be put to death. You must purge the evil from Israel.
(NIV)

Leviticus 20:13
13 " 'If a man lies with a man as one lies with a woman, both of them have done what is detestable. They must be put to death; their blood will be on their own heads.
(NIV)

Exodus 21:15
15 "Anyone who attacks his father or his mother must be put to death.
(NIV)

Clearly we can't follow these instructions from the Old Testament. So, if it is illegal for anyone, including MacArthur, to follow "all" of the old laws, then he must pick-and-choose which ones conform to his beliefs and are also not against the law.

It is an ironic choice of words to say that MacArthur would

pick-and-choose what parts of the Bible he wants to apply, because that is his own words to describe people who study the Old Testament and apply the New Testament.

In his article, "Our God-Breathed Bible," he writes,

> **The Pick-and-Choose Bible**
> *Some would like to remove certain verses from the Bible based on what they call "the spirit of Jesus." They say that whatever is in accordance with the spirit of Jesus should be included, and whatever does not should be taken out. For example, they would say the biblical injunction for capital punishment does not fit the spirit of Jesus because He was loving and gentle. Such people understand only one aspect of Jesus' nature. They do not understand He is also just and involved in judgment. They disregard anything that does not conform to their personal views.*
>
> *Jesus said, "Verily I say unto you, Till heaven and earth pass, one jot or one tittle shall in no way pass from the law, till all be fulfilled. Whosoever, therefore, shall break one of these least commandments, and shall teach men so, he shall be called least in the kingdom of heaven" (Matt. 5:18-19). He also said, "It is easier for heaven and earth to pass, than one tittle of the law to fail" (Luke 16:17). Even if the entire universe folds up, God's Word will remain because it is His Word (2 Pet. 1:20-21).*

I think it's odd to label the system of applying the New Testament and studying the Old Testament as "Pick-and-Choose."

But like he said, there are many things in the Old Testament that do not conform with the teachings of Jesus. That was one of the purposes of Jesus coming to earth. He came to save mankind from their own sins and to set forth the new agreement. The Bible is very clear on this.

Think about what makes more sense to you: to obey the new rules set forth by Jesus in the new agreement, thus ignoring conflicting rules of the old agreement ...
OR ...
Using old rules in the old agreement to justify ignoring the rules set out by Jesus in the new agreement.

Jesus made it clear that he was changing the old rules. Many times he used specific examples to get his point across. According to several verses in Matthew 5, Jesus explained that the old rule was not to murder but the new rule is to not even be angry with your brother. The old rule was not to commit adultery but the new rule is not to even think about it. The old rule was love your neighbor and hate your enemy but the new rule is love your enemy.

So it is clear that Jesus was changing the rules. The Old Testament prophesized this and the New Testament affirms it as well.

Consider this. You are an employer and you hire a person to be a janitor. You draw up an agreement that states that this person is to work four hours a day, Monday through Friday, and be paid the sum of $9 per hour. He signs the agreement and initials where he received the company handbook which explains how to conduct oneself as an employee of this company.

One year later, you promote him to stockroom manager and a new agreement is drawn up which states his new position, his new eight hours shifts, Tuesday through Saturday, and the pay will be $12 per hour. Again the agreement is signed by the employee and he initials where he received the company handbook.

Now we have two distinct singed agreements which have conflicting terms.

Could the employee decide to work Monday through Friday simply because he has a prior signed agreement that states this? Of course not.

Could the employer decide to still pay only $9 per hour because the old agreement states this? Again, of course not.

So the instructions for how to perform as an employee have changed but the rules of behavior laid out by the company handbook remain intact.

I once heard a preacher explain it this way. The Old Testament basically consists of three kinds of laws: municipal laws (the criminal and civil laws of the cities of the Old Testament), ceremonial laws, and moral laws.

We obviously would not follow the old municipal laws and we certainly wouldn't follow the old ceremonial laws like animal sacrifices. So that leaves the moral laws and those are covered by the Ten Commandments.

One of the favorite verses used by MacArthur and MacArthurian Christians is Matthew 5:18 which MacArthur uses in his article above.

> Matthew 5: 18
> I tell you the truth, until heaven and earth disappear, not the smallest letter, not the least stroke of a pen, will by any means disappear from the Law until everything is accomplished. (NIV)

This is one of their main arguments that the Old Testament should still be applied today.

But notice the wording - "disappear from the Law." Notice that it says, "the Law" as in singular, not "laws." It is also capitalized which means Jesus is referring to a specific law or set of laws. Which ones we don't even have to guess; we need only read the very first line of the very next verse.

Matthew 5:19

Anyone who breaks one of the least of these commandments and teaches others to do the same will be called least in the kingdom of heaven, but whoever practices and teaches these commands will be called great in the kingdom of heaven. (NIV)

So it is clear that Jesus is talking about the Ten Commandments. He says this with his own words. But this is not the only time Jesus made reference to keeping the Commandments.

Matthew 19:16-17

16 Now a man came up to Jesus and asked, "Teacher, what good thing must I do to get eternal life?"
17 "… If you want to enter life, obey the commandments." (NIV)

All the Ten Commandments are listed in the New Testament. Jesus mentions six of them in the following verse.

Matthew 19:18-19

18 "Which ones?" the man inquired. Jesus replied, " 'Do not murder, do not commit adultery, do not steal, do not give false testimony,
19 honor your father and mother,' and 'love your neighbor as yourself.'"
(NIV)

These represent Commandments five through ten. The first four can be found in other places of the New Testament.

Matthew 4:10 (Commandment One)
Jesus said to him, "Away from me, Satan! For it is written: 'Worship the Lord your God, and serve him only.'"
(NIV)

2. 1 Corinthians 10:14 (Commandment Two)
Therefore, my dear friends, flee from idolatry.
(NIV)

3. 1 Timothy 6 (Commandment Three)
All who are under the yoke of slavery should consider their masters worthy of full respect, so that God's name and our teaching may not be slandered.
(NIV)

Hebrews 4:9-10 (Commandment Four)
9 There remains, then, a Sabbath-rest for the people of God;
10 for anyone who enters God's rest also rests from his own work, just as God did from his
(NIV)

To me, the Bible is crystal clear. The new agreement gives us the new rules and tells us to keep the Commandments from the old agreement.

Chapter Three: Turn the Other Cheek

There is probably no other verse in the New Testament that has caused MacArthurian Christians more strife than Matthew 5:38-39.

> Matthew 5:38-39
> 38 You have heard that it was said, 'Eye for eye, and tooth for tooth.' 39 But I tell you, Do not resist an evil person. If someone strikes you on the right cheek, turn to him the other also.
> (NIV)

This simple message was part of the Sermon on the Mount and delivered to the disciples and followers by Jesus himself.

But the idea of turning the other cheek and resisting an evil person hardly conforms to the tough, aggressive Christian image that MacArthurian Christians try so hard to convey.

In MacArthur's article, "An Eye for an Eye, Part 2," he says:

Let's see how Jesus approaches it in verse 38 with a new instruction, a new principle. "But I tell you not to resist evil." That verse has been so misinterpreted. People think it is a reason for absolute pacifism, that we should say, "Go ahead, walk all over me. Abuse me, hit me, steal all I own. Go ahead, sin, we don't care. We're not going to resist evil, we'll just realize that evil is evil is evil, and it will do its thing.

Notice how MacArthur takes a simple idea like, "If someone strikes you on the right cheek," and changes it to things like "walk all over me", "abuse me", and "steal all I own." Changing the words to harsher acts of violence certainly makes it easier to sell the belief that you shouldn't let it happen.

But when this verse says, "Do not resist an evil person," we don't have to assume that it means to resist all evil in the world. We don't have to guess at all because it explains that the evil person is simply someone hitting you on the cheek.

MacArthur takes it further in his article, "The Actions of Kingdom Love."

> *There are people who laugh at this and they say it's ridiculous. If somebody comes up and, you know, punches me in the face, I'm not going to say, "Here, hit the other side." That's just not normal because built into us there are self-defense mechanisms that God has given us for the sake of self-preservation. And I agree with that. This is not about that. This is not about having somebody mug you at night somewhere when you're in a vulnerable position and you are lying down and say, "Oh, kick me again, kick me again, this is virtue, this is virtue." It's not about that.*

Now "someone strikes you on the right cheek" has become "having someone mug you at night somewhere when you're in a vulnerable position and you are lying down."

Notice how he also uses "self-defense mechanisms that God

has given us" as another reason to promote the idea that the words Jesus used here were about something totally different.

I find this very odd. Jesus is instructing his disciples, his followers, and Christians today, to turn the other cheek if someone strikes you. And MacArthur says here, "If somebody comes up and, you know, punches me in the face, I'm not going to say, 'Here, hit the other side.'"

As a man, I understand his reasoning here, It's just not in our nature as humans.

But that is exactly what Jesus said to do. He did not say, "If someone walks all over you." He did not say, "If someone steals all you own." He did not say anything about being mugged at night while you're in a vulnerable position and laying down. He used a very specific phrase, "If someone strikes you on your right cheek."

Throughout the New Testament, Jesus is setting the course of actions for all Christians and many times he references old rules to emphasize the new rules. This is one of those occasions.

Notice that Jesus begins by saying, "You have heard that it was said…"

Have we heard it before? Is it mentioned in the Old Testament?

Yes it is - three times.

Exodus 22-25

22 If men who are fighting hit a pregnant woman and she gives birth prematurely but there is no serious injury, the offender must be fined whatever the woman's husband demands and the court allows.

23 But if there is serious injury, you are to take life for life,

24 eye for eye, tooth for tooth, hand for hand, foot for foot,

25 burn for burn, wound for wound, bruise for bruise.

(NIV)

Leviticus 24: 19-20

19 If anyone injures his neighbor, whatever he has done must be done to him:

20 fracture for fracture, eye for eye, tooth for tooth. As he has injured the other, so he is to be injured.

(NIV)

Deuteronomy 19:19-21

19 then do to him as he intended to do to his brother. You must purge the evil from among you.

20 The rest of the people will hear of this and be afraid, and never again will such an evil thing be done among you.

21 Show no pity: life for life, eye for eye, tooth for tooth, hand for hand, foot for foot.

(NIV)

Two of these are dealing with someone actually trying to hurt his neighbor or brother and one speaks directly of men involved in a fist fight.

After referencing the three places in the Old Testament where the old rule is written, the words of Jesus make perfect sense.

Changing the words of Jesus into harsher crimes would make it easier to refute but MacArthur also teaches that this verse was not even intended for us today, but for his followers back then for getting thrown out of the church..

Picking up where we left off in MacArthur's article, "The Actions of Kingdom Love," he says:

> *What is it about? Jesus said in John 16, right after John 15 that I quoted earlier, "The time is going to come when they throw you out of the synagogue." He was telling His followers that, they're going to throw you out of the synagogue. We talked about that last Sunday. And they did. They were unsynagogued. That was not a small deal because Jewish society circled around the synagogue that was both the circumference and core of life. The greatest single humiliation, the greatest shame was to be excommunicated from the synagogue. You were then constituted as a reprobate, very serious. And they took it very seriously.*

My simple argument would be this: If Jesus was talking about being thrown out of a church, why wouldn't he simply say that instead of, "If someone strikes you on the right cheek."

Continuing in "The Actions of Kingdom Love."

> *When someone was unsynagogued, which they were for their faith in Jesus Christ, frequently they were whipped before whoever wanted to watch. Clothes were taken of their backs and they received 39 lashes, leather thongs probably imbedded with bits of stone which lacerated their backs 39 times. The Apostle Paul in 2 Corinthians 11:24 says, "They did it to me five times." Five times the Jews did it to me. Acts 5:40 talks about those in the early church who preached the gospel being flogged. That was the physical punishment connected to the shame of being unsynagogued for the sake of Jesus Christ.*

Again, my simple argument would be this: If Jesus was talking about receiving 39 lashes, why wouldn't he simply say that instead of, "If someone strikes you on the right cheek."

More from "The Actions of Kingdom Love."

> *But there was something else that they did. The way you dishonored someone, one of the ways you dishonored someone was to slap them across the face. And while there was a real flogging, actual physical pain, there was also a symbolic humiliation in front of the synagogue congregation. One of the officials would slap the person across the face as a symbolic indignity and humiliation. That's what's in view here. When they bring you in front to humiliate you and they slap you across the face, offer the other cheek, accept your humiliation.*

So according to John MacArthur, not only does "strikes you

on your right cheek" apparently mean any form of aggression other than someone actually striking you on the right cheek, he now seems to say that these words from Jesus was not even meant for modern day Christians, but was instead meant for people 2000 years ago who attended the churches of the Pharisees and were being punished for having faith in Jesus.

This entire proposal seems completely strange to me. The Pharisees were the enemy of Jesus. They did not accept him for who he claimed to be and they were instrumental in getting him crucified. Jesus had many harsh words for the Pharisees.

To try to sum up what MacArthur appears to be teaching about Matthew 5:38-39, if you were around 2000 years ago, were attending the church of the Pharisees, were brave enough to announce your faith in Jesus, and were being punished via flogging or a humiliating slap to the face by these Godless hypocrites that hated Jesus and had him killed, you deserve what you're getting and should not only take it in stride, but request more punishment.

It doesn't quite make sense, does it?

The thing is, if you're going to study the words of Jesus, then you should use the words of Jesus. If you're going to study Matthew 5:38-39, then use the words in Matthew 5:38-39.

As muggings go, I also believe one should defend themselves

anytime they are in danger. Jesus never said otherwise. But muggings have nothing to do with the words of Jesus in Matthew 5:38-39 and if you make that connection, if you change the meaning of the words or change the words themselves, you are no longer studying the words of Jesus.

So let's look at the actual words, "If someone strikes you on the right cheek, turn to him the other also."

I don't know how many of you have actually been struck by another person, but I have. It was no big deal. It was designed to lure me into a fight and I was too weak to resist.

That's right, being drawn into the fight was an act of weakness and refraining from it would have taken more strength, strength that at the time I couldn't find.

When I make this argument to students of MacArthur, they demonstrate how well they have learned MacArthur's techniques.

"I suppose if terrorists attack us again, we're supposed to hug them and pat them on the back?"

"If someone kills your mother, are you going to bake them a cake?"

"If someone rapes your daughter, are you going to offer them your wife as well?"

These are some actual arguments made by MacArthurian Christians when discussing Matthew 5:38-39 on the message boards. And the more you try to focus on the actual words of Jesus, the more exaggerated the hypothetical 'what ifs' become.

When I said, "Forget about terrorists, murderers, and rapists for a second and just answer this question - As a Christian, what would you do if someone simply hit you on your cheek?"

I've never had one MacArthurian Christian who could answer that simple question. Nor have I ever come across the answer from MacArthur's writings.

But I reiterate, Matthew 5:38-39 does not address any of these criminal acts. Criminal acts should be dealt with by man's laws. Even the Bible says so. Someone hitting you on the cheek is also against the law and pressing charges would not be out of the question nor do I believe it goes against what Jesus is saying here.

Seriously, read the actual words. Is it so hard to believe that Jesus meant exactly what he said? Let me ask that again. Is it so hard to believe that Jesus meant exactly what he said?

If someone actually strikes you on the cheek to lure you into a fight, be the bigger person and resist temptation to be drawn into a fight where someone might actually get hurt. Why is that so hard to believe? What has ever been settled by a fist fight?

Aren't Christians supposed to set the examples for mankind? Aren't Christians the ones to rise above?

What kind of person would retaliate if struck on the cheek by another person? Sounds like a silly question, doesn't it? The answer is almost everyone: drinkers, drug users, thieves, murderers, prisoners, rapists, atheists, evil people, school teachers, bus drivers, architects, veterinarians, veterans, vegetarians, etc., could all easily fit into that category.

So what then would separate Christians from anyone else? This is a question I ask myself a lot when studying MacArthur's teachings. If everything MacArthur preaches is true, when it comes to how a Christian is supposed to conduct themselves, what is the difference in a Christian and everyone else?

Throughout the New Testament, all the teachings of Jesus have a uniform message of compassion, forgiveness and love. This verse has the same exact message.

So read the words of Jesus with your heart. He did not make this passage so hard to understand that you need to have someone explain it to you. If you change the words and the meaning, are you really doing it because you think you know what Jesus was saying better than the people who wrote the gospels, or is it simply because it makes you feel better about your own human frailties?

Jesus gave instructions to Christians on how to live and act as Christians. These instructions are not easy. Most times they are in direct contradiction to what our human mind and proverbial heart says is normal.

But that's what separates Christians from non-Christians.

If someone tries to hurt you, defend yourself. If someone commits a criminal act against you, do everything within the law to see that they are brought to justice.

But if someone simply tries to antagonize you by striking you on the cheek, be the bigger person as Jesus instructed. Be the stronger person. Be the better person.

Be the Christian.

Chapter Four: Judging

The Sermon on the Mount continues in Matthew 7 and begins with yet another obstacle for the MacArthurian Christian. But MacArthur has a explanation for that as well.

> Matthew 7- 1:2
> 1 "Do not judge, or you too will be judged.
> 2 For in the same way you judge others, you will be judged, and with the measure you use, it will be measured to you."
> (NIV)

In his article, "Stop Criticizing," MacArthur writes:

> *This morning I want to encourage you if you will, with me, to turn in your Bible to Matthew, chapter 7. Matthew 7, beginning at verse 1. "Judge not, that ye be not judged. For with what judgment ye judge, ye shall be judged: and with what measure ye measure, it shall be measured to you again...*
>
> *Now, this is a fascinating portion of Scripture, a Scripture that is frequently referred to and oft quoted, and yet sometimes not really put together in a total package as the Lord, I believe, intended for it to be.*

Do you see a pattern with John MacArthur? He starts by taking the very simple words of Jesus, which is then followed by him explaining what Jesus REALLY intended. Amazingly, it seems many times to me that, according to MacArthur, what Jesus really intended turns out to be 180 degrees opposite of what he said.

Once again, he sets the tone for explaining that this message delivered to his disciples and his followers had to do with the scribes and the Pharisees.

More from the article "Stop Criticizing."

> *Now, as in all the other elements of the Sermon on the Mount, the perspective here is given in contrast to the view of the scribes and the Pharisees.*

So according to MacArthur, when Jesus tells his disciples and his followers not to judge, he's giving instructions to the scribes and Pharisees, people not even there at the moment.

Here's the message that Jesus is sending to the scribes and Pharisees, according to MacArthur. Again from the article, "Stop Criticizing."

> *In other words, you think you've got the answers. You think you've got the system. You think you're the judges. But you're wrong.*

So according to MacArthur, Jesus is telling the scribes and Pharisees that they are not the judges. And why are they not the judges? Still, from "Stop Criticizing."

> *In other words, they made judgments, but their judgments were wrong. They sat as condemning,*

critical judges of other people. This is the one thing that marked their relations with others: a judgmental, condemning attitude.

Again, according to MacArthur, they are not the judges because their judgments were condemning, critical, wrong, and the one I like the most, judgmental.

So if the scribes and Pharisees are not the judges, who is? According to MacArthur, Christians are the judges and are supposed to judge others.

Still from "Stop Criticizing."

And so some people have taken "judge not" and just fit it into the mentality of the time. But the Lord is not condemning law courts. I mean, the Bible instituted that. The principle of an eye for an eye and a tooth for a tooth is based upon a law court, and Romans 13 affirms the right for a nation to rule its people. And the Bible is not condemning any kind of judging or discriminating. The Bible tells us, as believers, that we must discern. Right? That we must know the truth from the falsehood.

There are so many things to mention in this paragraph that it's hard to know where to begin.

First, judging people has nothing to do with a court of law. When Jesus says "judge not," he's telling Christians not to judge a person's heart. In other words, it's not our place, nor do we have the authority, to say that someone else will not be saved or doesn't deserved to be saved.

Nor is Jesus suggesting that we do away with criminal laws and courts and jails and punishment. In fact, the Bible mentions many times the necessity of man's law and the courts.

But it seems that this is how MacArthur chooses to set the tone for promoting personal judgment. He even uses an Old Testament law as an example. We have already determined that MacArthur has concluded that the Old Testament is for application, albeit which parts we can't be sure, but this particular law he's mentioning was one of those specifically reversed by Jesus.

Matthew 5:38-39
38"You have heard that it was said, 'Eye for eye, and tooth for tooth.' 39But I tell you, Do not resist an evil person. If someone strikes you on the right cheek, turn to him the other also.
(NIV)

It makes me wonder why he would use "eye for an eye" to justify judgment or anything else since this is a rule that Jesus specifically said doesn't apply anymore.

And then this line, "And the Bible is not condemning any kind of judging or discriminating."

Wait a minute. MacArthur is saying that the Bible is not condemning ANY KIND of judging? But it must be condemning some kind of judging since the words are, "Do not judge."

And didn't MacArthur just say that Jesus was telling the Pharisees they were not the judges because their judgment was too condemning, critical, wrong and judgmental? So clearly, according to MacArthur's earlier comments, some judging was condemned.

Anytime you read something and try to make the words mean something other than what they say, it's easy to end up contradicting yourself somewhere. It's like trying to prove that two plus two equals six. You can write it down that way, but it doesn't hold up to simple math. And to me, MacArthur's words do not hold up to the simple words of Jesus.

Then there's this line, "The Bible tells us, as believers, that we must discern. Right?"

MacArthur does this quite often. The Bible says many times that we are to discern and everywhere it says that, MacArthur and MacArthurian Christians use that as evidence that Christians are to judge others.

But are "judging" and "discerning" the same thing? Of course not. They're not even close.

40

Discern
to recognize or identify as separate and distinct :
DISCRIMINATE <discern right from wrong>
(Merriam-Webster online dictionary)

Judge
to form an estimate or evaluation of; especially : to form a
negative opinion about <shouldn't judge him because of his
accent>
(Merriam-Webster online dictionary)

We can clearly see by the definitions that these are indeed two very separate things. To identify right from wrong has absolutely nothing to do with judging someone. Nothing!

To go through the Bible and use verses where it talks about discerning and use that as evidence that we should judge, I believe to be a very misleading thing to do.

To try to prove that Christians are supposed to judge others, MacArthur doesn't just correlate two words with different meanings, he uses other verses as well

Many MacArthurian Christians have used 1 Corinthians 6:2 to justify judging others.

1 Corinthians 6:2
Do you not know that the saints will judge the world? And if

you are to judge the world, are you not competent to judge trivial cases?
(NIV)

The irony here is that Paul, in his words to the church in Corinth, really is talking about judging as in a court of law. He's saying if church members have a dispute, don't take it before the courts, you are qualified to make that decision. In other words, let's keep it in house.

When Jesus speaks about judging people's hearts, MacArthur makes a connection to the legal system to make his claim, and when Paul make a reference to the legal system, MacArthur changes it to mean judging people's hearts.

But the first part of 1 Corinthians 6:2 does talk about that kind of judgment. "Do you not know that the saints will judge the world?"

Paul does say that the "saints" will judge the world. He even goes further and tells the people of this church that this means them. "If you are to judge the world..."

So the questions is: who are the saints?

I think it's clear that the saints and the "Elect" or the same. We will talk more about the Elect in a later chapter. So the real question is - who are the Elect?

MacArthur teaches that the Elect is everyone who will be saved and those people were chosen before God created the world.

I believe also they were chosen (or elected) before God created the world but I believe they make up a small percentage of everyone saved and that everyone has the free will to choose God and be saved.

But whoever the saints are that will judge the world, it talks about them in Revelation.

> Revelation 20:4
> I saw thrones on which were seated those who had been given authority to judge. And I saw the souls of those who had been beheaded because of their testimony for Jesus and because of the word of God. They had not worshiped the beast or his image and had not received his mark on their foreheads or their hands. They came to life and reigned with Christ a thousand years.
> (NIV)

My problem with MacArthur's theory that everyone who will be saved was pre-chosen before creation, it makes me wonder then who is being judged here. Who would even need to be judged if everything was determined before the world was created. For that matter, why did Jesus even have to come to die for our sins if it was already decided? Furthermore, why did Jesus and Paul try so hard to save so many people if things were already decided?

It doesn't make sense to me. But Revelation 20:4 explains who will be judged. "The rest of the dead did not come to life until the thousand years were ended." And how is everyone else judged? It explains that also in Revelation 20.

> Revelation 20:12-13
>
> 12And I saw the dead, great and small, standing before the throne, and books were opened. Another book was opened, which is the book of life. The dead were judged according to what they had done as recorded in the books. 13The sea gave up the dead that were in it, and death and Hades gave up the dead that were in them, and each person was judged according to what he had done.
>
> (NIV)

There are people who believe that faith alone will bring salvation. But you can that it says twice here, and very clearly, that each person is judged by "what they had done."

So when Paul was speaking to the members of the church of Corinth, he was calling them saints. It's not hard to believe that the members of this church, or at least some of them, will make up part of the Elect. They were preaching the gospel of Jesus when it was a very dangerous thing to do. People were beheaded in those days for preaching Christianity.

44

It says that also in Revelation 20:4. "And I saw the souls of those who had been beheaded because of their testimony for Jesus and because of the word of God."

Where Jesus was teaching his disciples and followers to judge not, MacArthur says that Jesus wasn't even talking to them (or us), but instead was giving instructions to the scribes and Pharisees.

Yet when Paul was writing directly to a specific group of people, MacArthur makes it sound like Paul was speaking to us all.

But let's make several hypothetical assumptions. Let's assume that MacArthur is correct that we don't have free will to choose to live by God's word but everything was decided for us long ago. And let's even assume MacArthur is correct that everyone saved makes up the Elect or saints. That would mean MacArthur is correct that Paul was speaking to us all instead of just the people of this church.

If all of this were true, it still doesn't instruct Christians to judge people. Look at the wording. "Do you not know that the saints WILL judge the world? And if you ARE TO judge the world…" It says the saints WILL judge – as in the future. It says if you ARE TO judge – also meaning the future. And that coincides perfectly with Revelation. The saints WILL judge at that time.

Another favorite of MacArthurian Christians is John 7:24

John 7:24
Judge not according to the appearance, but judge righteous judgment.
KJB

This has been thrown at me many times to justify a Christian's responsibility to judge.

In "Stop Criticizing," MacArthur writes,

> **To go around saying, "Well, we should love everybody and never judge anybody," that isn't what the Lord is saying.**

That's odd because I think that's exactly what the Lord is saying. He even instructs us to love our enemies.

Still in "Stop Criticizing"

> *Jesus expressed such evaluation. He condemned repeatedly. He judged, He evaluated, He criticized.*

The Bible never says that Jesus or God should not judge, only that we shouldn't.

Still in "Stop Criticizing"

We must judge. We must evaluate. Romans 16:17 says, "We must mark them that cause divisions and offenses contrary to the doctrine which we've learned and avoid them." We must make doctrinal distinctions, and we must mark the people who offend that doctrine, and we must avoid those people. We can't all get together. We must make distinctions. And that judgment must begin, says, Peter, at the house of God. We have a right to judge righteous judgment. John 7:24.

If you read all of John 7, you will see that Jesus had just healed a man on a Sunday and the Jews looking on were angry for him doing this on a Sabbath. Jesus tells them that if you can circumcise a boy on the Sabbath and that is not against the law of Moses, then healing the whole body of a man on a Sabbath is nothing to be angry about. So he says to stop judging by appearances and judge righteous judgment.

To take this verse and try to say that Jesus is telling us that it's ok to judge others as long as we use righteous judgment doesn't make sense. If that were true, then Jesus is telling the Jews that they can judge Him. Do you think the Jews that were there that day were qualified to judge Jesus?

Jesus is talking about His actions. He's telling them that if you're going to judge an action, do it correctly. We are supposed to know what actions are right and wrong. That has nothing to do with judging a person.

Until I met a MacArthurian Christian, I never heard anyone try so hard to explain Matthew 7:1. In fact, I never met anyone who felt the need to try to explain this verse. Any average person knows exactly what is being discussed and what kind of judging is being talked about. So I couldn't understand the lengths MacArthurian Christians would go to just to debate this verse, be it talking about a court of law or deciding what college to attend.

But judging isn't simply a conscious decision about who deserves to be saved or whose souls should be condemned. Judging is also feeling in your heart that another person's sins are worse than your own. And I think we are all guilty of that.

For example, I have heard many more sermons and read many more Christian articles on homosexuality than I have about lying. Yet homosexuality is practiced by a small portion of the population and I believe we are all guilty of lying, if nothing more than a little white lie occasionally. And lying is mentioned many more times in the Bible than homosexuality and is even one of the Ten Commandments. But it's easy for us to feel in our hearts that one sin might be worse than the other.

That is also judging.

No matter how you twist it, Jesus gave his disciples, his followers, and us, specific instructions to "judge not."

Chapter Five: The Sermon on the Mount

The Sermon on the Mount is the longest collection of the teachings of Jesus in the Bible. Let's look at in its entirety.

Matthew 5

The Beatitudes

1Now when he saw the crowds, he went up on a mountainside and sat down. His disciples came to him, 2and he began to teach them saying:

3"Blessed are the poor in spirit,
for theirs is the kingdom of heaven.
4Blessed are those who mourn,
for they will be comforted.
5Blessed are the meek,
for they will inherit the earth.
6Blessed are those who hunger and thirst for righteousness,
for they will be filled.
7Blessed are the merciful,
for they will be shown mercy.
8Blessed are the pure in heart,
for they will see God.
9Blessed are the peacemakers,
for they will be called sons of God.
10Blessed are those who are persecuted because of righteousness,
for theirs is the kingdom of heaven.

11"Blessed are you when people insult you, persecute you and falsely say all kinds of evil against you because of me. 12Rejoice and be glad, because great is your reward in heaven, for in the same way they persecuted the prophets who were before you.

Salt and Light

13"You are the salt of the earth. But if the salt loses its saltiness, how can it be made salty again? It is no longer good for anything, except to be thrown out and trampled by men. 14"You are the light of the world. A city on a hill cannot be hidden. 15Neither do people light a lamp and put it under a bowl. Instead they put it on its stand, and it gives light to everyone in the house. 16In the same way, let your light shine before men, that they may see your good deeds and praise your Father in heaven.

The Fulfillment of the Law

17"Do not think that I have come to abolish the Law or the Prophets; I have not come to abolish them but to fulfill them. 18I tell you the truth, until heaven and earth disappear, not the smallest letter, not the least stroke of a pen, will by any means disappear from the Law until everything is accomplished. 19Anyone who breaks one of the least of these commandments and teaches others to do the same will be called least in the kingdom of heaven, but whoever practices and teaches these commands will be called great in the kingdom of heaven.

20For I tell you that unless your righteousness surpasses that of the Pharisees and the teachers of the law, you will certainly not enter the kingdom of heaven.

Murder

21"You have heard that it was said to the people long ago, 'Do not murder,[a] and anyone who murders will be subject to judgment.' 22But I tell you that anyone who is angry with his brother[b]will be subject to judgment. Again, anyone who says to his brother, 'Raca,[c]' is answerable to the Sanhedrin. But anyone who says, 'You fool!' will be in danger of the fire of hell.
23"Therefore, if you are offering your gift at the altar and there remember that your brother has something against you, 24leave your gift there in front of the altar. First go and be reconciled to your brother; then come and offer your gift.
25"Settle matters quickly with your adversary who is taking you to court. Do it while you are still with him on the way, or he may hand you over to the judge, and the judge may hand you over to the officer, and you may be thrown into prison. 26I tell you the truth, you will not get out until you have paid the last penny.[d]

Adultery

27"You have heard that it was said, 'Do not commit adultery.'[e] 28But I tell you that anyone who looks at a woman lustfully has already committed adultery with her in his heart. 29If your right eye causes you to sin, gouge it out and throw it away. It is better for you to lose one part of your body than for your whole body to be thrown into hell. 30And if your right hand causes you to sin, cut it off and throw it away. It is better for you to lose one part of your body than for your whole body to go into hell.

Divorce

31"It has been said, 'Anyone who divorces his wife must give her a certificate of divorce.'[f] 32But I tell you that anyone who divorces his wife, except for marital unfaithfulness, causes her to become an adulteress, and anyone who marries the divorced woman commits adultery.

Oaths

33"Again, you have heard that it was said to the people long ago, 'Do not break your oath, but keep the oaths you have made to the Lord.' 34But I tell you, Do not swear at all: either by heaven, for it is God's throne; 35or by the earth, for it is his footstool; or by Jerusalem, for it is the city of the Great King. 36And do not swear by your head, for you cannot make even one hair white or black. 37Simply let your 'Yes' be 'Yes,' and your 'No,' 'No'; anything beyond this comes from the evil one.

An Eye for an Eye

38"You have heard that it was said, 'Eye for eye, and tooth for tooth.'[g] 39But I tell you, Do not resist an evil person. If someone strikes you on the right cheek, turn to him the other also. 40And if someone wants to sue you and take your tunic, let him have your cloak as well. 41If someone forces you to go one mile, go with him two miles. 42Give to the one who asks you, and do not turn away from the one who wants to borrow from you.

Love for Enemies

43"You have heard that it was said, 'Love your neighbor[h] and hate your enemy.' 44But I tell you: Love your enemies[i] and pray for those who persecute you, 45that you may be sons of your Father in heaven. He causes his sun to rise on the evil and the good, and sends rain on the righteous and the unrighteous. 46If you love those who love you, what reward will you get? Are not even the tax collectors doing that? 47And if you greet only your brothers, what are you doing more than others? Do not even pagans do that? 48Be perfect, therefore, as your heavenly Father is perfect.

Matthew 6

Giving to the Needy

1"Be careful not to do your 'acts of righteousness' before men, to be seen by them. If you do, you will have no reward from your Father in heaven.

  2"So when you give to the needy, do not announce it with trumpets, as the hypocrites do in the synagogues and on the streets, to be honored by men. I tell you the truth, they have received their reward in full. 3But when you give to the needy, do not let your left hand know what your right hand is doing, 4so that your giving may be in secret. Then your Father, who sees what is done in secret, will reward you.

Prayer

5"And when you pray, do not be like the hypocrites, for they love to pray standing in the synagogues and on the street corners to be seen by men. I tell you the truth, they have received their reward in full. 6But when you pray, go into your room, close the door and pray to your Father, who is unseen. Then your Father, who sees what is done in secret, will reward you. 7And when you pray, do not keep on babbling like pagans, for they think they will be heard because of their many words. 8Do not be like them, for your Father knows what you need before you ask him.

9"This, then, is how you should pray:

  "'Our Father in heaven,
  hallowed be your name,
10your kingdom come,
  your will be done
    on earth as it is in heaven.

11Give us today our daily bread.

12Forgive us our debts,

    as we also have forgiven our debtors.

13And lead us not into temptation, but deliver us from the evil one.[a]' 14For if you forgive men when they sin against you, your heavenly Father will also forgive you. 15But if you do not forgive men their sins, your Father will not forgive your sins.

Fasting

16"When you fast, do not look somber as the hypocrites do, for they disfigure their faces to show men they are fasting. I tell you the truth, they have received their reward in full. 17But when you fast, put oil on your head and wash your face, 18so that it will not be obvious to men that you are fasting, but only to your Father, who is unseen; and your Father, who sees what is done in secret, will reward you.

Treasures in Heaven

19"Do not store up for yourselves treasures on earth, where moth and rust destroy, and where thieves break in and steal. 20But store up for yourselves treasures in heaven, where moth and rust do not destroy, and where thieves do not break in and steal. 21For where your treasure is, there your heart will be also.

22"The eye is the lamp of the body. If your eyes are good,

your whole body will be full of light. 23But if your eyes are bad, your whole body will be full of darkness. If then the light within you is darkness, how great is that darkness!

24"No one can serve two masters. Either he will hate the one and love the other, or he will be devoted to the one and despise the other. You cannot serve both God and Money.

Do Not Worry

25"Therefore I tell you, do not worry about your life, what you will eat or drink; or about your body, what you will wear. Is not life more important than food, and the body more important than clothes? 26Look at the birds of the air; they do not sow or reap or store away in barns, and yet your heavenly Father feeds them. Are you not much more valuable than they? 27Who of you by worrying can add a single hour to his life[b]?

28"And why do you worry about clothes? See how the lilies of the field grow. They do not labor or spin. 29Yet I tell you that not even Solomon in all his splendor was dressed like one of these. 30If that is how God clothes the grass of the field, which is here today and tomorrow is thrown into the fire, will he not much more clothe you, O you of little faith? 31So do not worry, saying, 'What shall we eat?' or 'What shall we drink?' or 'What shall we wear?' 32For the pagans run after all these things, and your heavenly Father knows that you need them. 33But seek first his kingdom and his righteousness, and all these things will be given to you as well. 34Therefore do not worry about tomorrow, for tomorrow will worry about itself. Each day has enough trouble of its own.

Matthew 7

Judging Others

1"Do not judge, or you too will be judged. 2For in the same way you judge others, you will be judged, and with the measure you use, it will be measured to you.
3"Why do you look at the speck of sawdust in your brother's eye and pay no attention to the plank in your own eye? 4How can you say to your brother, 'Let me take the speck out of your eye,' when all the time there is a plank in your own eye? 5You hypocrite, first take the plank out of your own eye, and then you will see clearly to remove the speck from your brother's eye.
6"Do not give dogs what is sacred; do not throw your pearls to pigs. If you do, they may trample them under their feet, and then turn and tear you to pieces.

Ask, Seek, Knock

7"Ask and it will be given to you; seek and you will find; knock and the door will be opened to you. 8For everyone who asks receives; he who seeks finds; and to him who knocks, the door will be opened.
9"Which of you, if his son asks for bread, will give him a stone? 10Or if he asks for a fish, will give him a snake? 11If

you, then, though you are evil, know how to give good gifts to your children, how much more will your Father in heaven give good gifts to those who ask him! 12So in everything, do to others what you would have them do to you, for this sums up the Law and the Prophets.

The Narrow and Wide Gates

13"Enter through the narrow gate. For wide is the gate and broad is the road that leads to destruction, and many enter through it. 14But small is the gate and narrow the road that leads to life, and only a few find it.

A Tree and Its Fruit

15"Watch out for false prophets. They come to you in sheep's clothing, but inwardly they are ferocious wolves. 16By their fruit you will recognize them. Do people pick grapes from thornbushes, or figs from thistles? 17Likewise every good tree bears good fruit, but a bad tree bears bad fruit. 18A good tree cannot bear bad fruit, and a bad tree cannot bear good fruit. 19Every tree that does not bear good fruit is cut down and thrown into the fire. 20Thus, by their fruit you will recognize them.

21"Not everyone who says to me, 'Lord, Lord,' will enter the kingdom of heaven, but only he who does the will of my Father who is in heaven. 22Many will say to me on that day, 'Lord, Lord, did we not prophesy in your name, and in your name drive out demons and perform many miracles?' 23Then I will tell them plainly, 'I never knew you. Away from me, you evildoers!'

The Wise and Foolish Builders

24"Therefore everyone who hears these words of mine and puts them into practice is like a wise man who built his house on the rock. 25The rain came down, the streams rose, and the winds blew and beat against that house; yet it did not fall, because it had its foundation on the rock. 26But everyone who hears these words of mine and does not put them into practice is like a foolish man who built his house on sand. 27The rain came down, the streams rose, and the winds blew and beat against that house, and it fell with a great crash." 28When Jesus had finished saying these things, the crowds were amazed at his teaching, 29because he taught as one who had authority, and not as their teachers of the law. (NIV)

This is the heart of the message Jesus brought to us. What does MacArthur say about the Sermon on the Mount?

In his article, "Examine Yourself," he says:

> *If you want to know if you're a Christian, compare your life with the standard Christ presents in the Sermon on the Mount.*

MacArthur is saying to use the Sermon on the Mount as a standard to see if you are a Christian. But which parts of the Sermon on the Mount does he say we should follow and for what time period does it really apply?

In "The Beatitudes: Happy are the Humble," he writes:

> **Every principle in the Sermon on the Mount is found elsewhere in the New Testament. For that reason as well as the reasons given above, Christ's message must be for us now.**

I'm confused. If every principle of the Sermon is important and it applies to us now, why then does MacArthur go to great lengths to try to convince us that "judge not" and "turn the other cheek" do not apply to us today but instead applies to the scribes and Pharisees from 2000 years ago?

Can you see the problem you get into when trying to say that certain words or phrases mean something other than what they say? It's hard for me to understand someone saying in one place that the entire Sermon on the Mount applies to us today but then also go to great lengths to make us believe that we don't have to follow the one in there about judging and that one in there about turning the other cheek because those were meant for someone else so just ignore those.

It's doesn't seem right. Either they all apply to us or they don't. You can't simply throw out some of them because they cramp your style.

What does MacArthur say was the purpose of the Sermon on the Mount?

In "The Beatitudes: Happiness Is . . . .," here's what he had to say:

> **The happiness of believers is one of Christ's main concerns. That is evident because Jesus' first recorded sermon (the Sermon on the Mount) begins with the theme of happiness.**

And again, in "The Beatitudes: Happy are the Humble," he writes:

> **Jesus came to earth to bring men happiness. The key to experiencing the happiness (or blessedness) spoken of in the Beatitudes (Matt. 5:3-12) is in following a new standard of living. That standard is set forth in the Sermon on the Mount.**

I like this message. MacArthur is saying that the Sermon on the Mount, at least the beginning, was all about happiness, and that "Jesus came to earth to bring men happiness." I really like that.

He says also that if you want to know if you're a Christian, compare yourself to the principles found in the Sermon on the Mount. I like that too.

It nice to see MacArthur be so positive and uplifting about something.

But in the article "In The Way to Heaven," he writes:

> *There are many people who through the years have assumed that the Sermon on the Mount was some kind of statement about noble ethics which if a man follows will cause him to earn eternal life. Nothing could be further from the truth. The sermon was an all-out attack on salvation by religious ceremony or by religious effort or by human works.*

Wow! Now the Sermon on the Mount is not a list of principles to follow. And so much for the reason Jesus delivered the sermon being to bring happiness. Now "the sermon was an all-out attack on salvation by religious ceremony."

An all-out attack?

When I read this wonderful sermon, I only see a wonderful, positive message. I don't see an attack.

Chapter Six: Anger and Aggression

Going back to when I first became aware of the teachings of John MacArthur, it was on an on line Christian forum where Christians of all denominations, or no denomination, could post questions and comments and debate their views. Almost every poster was respectful and pleasant, except two.

These two were much more aggressive and anytime someone posted something they disagreed with, which was very often, they went on the attack. The would post a response to the other Christian who posted something contrary to their belief and call them "idiot", "fool", "moron", and a host of other names I cannot list here.

When others would try to explain that this behavior was not Christian, they attacked more. They pointed out that Jesus also called people names and since he never sinned, calling people names must not be a sin.

I disagree. Jesus referred to some people as "fools" or "hypocrites," but with Jesus, it wasn't a matter of immature name calling, Jesus could actually see into their hearts and know how to identify them. This is not a gift that God choose to bless us with.

One of the MacArthurian Christians also explained that it was a Christian's duty to be the aggressor. He offered the salt parable from the Sermon on the Mount. "We are supposed to be like salt and when salt is poured into an open wound, it stings "

I had never heard that translation of the wonderful "salt of the earth" parable. Let's look at it again.

> Matthew 5:13-14
> 13"You are the salt of the earth. But if the salt loses its saltiness, how can it be made salty again? It is no longer good for anything, except to be thrown out and trampled by men. (NIV)

I tried to explain that is was a metaphor, not to be confused with actual grains of salt. Just like the next verse says you are the light of the world, it too is a metaphor. It doesn't mean you have the same physical characteristics as an incandescent bulb.

I have always believed these verses to be a simple to understand metaphor. Salt was used to purify. Jesus is saying that you (Christians) are the salt (the pure) of the world. But if you lose your faith, what good are you? You're then the same as everyone else.

When I began studying some of the words of MacArthur, I now know where they got this idea.

In this passage from "You are the Salt of the Earth," MacArthur first talks about these verses in the same manner as I just did, but then he adds this:

Let me give you a third option. Salt stings. Not only is it white and adds flavor, it has a medicinal or healing property when put into a wound. So some say that the Lord is saying, "Believers are not to be honey to soothe the sinful world, you are to be salt in the world, so whenever you see a place where there is a problem, you should just throw yourselves in and make it sting." I like that. I don't think we do near enough of that. I think we just want to drip honey on everyone, and we figure that if we never offend, if we just go along in life, it will be alright. If we gloss it over and let it be the way it is, nobody will get upset and everyone will say, "Oh, those Christians are so loving and tolerant of us." But there is never a clear definition of a distinction, you see. We're not honey, we're salt.

MacArthurian Christians have learned this well – "throw yourself in and make it sting."

Sometimes the MacArthurian Christians would defend their actions by saying that they were being persecuted for their beliefs and had to retaliate. Here I would point out one of my favorites.

Matthew 5:12-12
11"Blessed are you when people insult you, persecute you and falsely say all kinds of evil against you because of me. 12Rejoice and be glad, because great is your reward in heaven,

for in the same way they persecuted the prophets who were before you.
(NIV)

"Rejoice and be glad" even when people are falsely saying all kinds of evil against you. "Rejoice and be glad."

The MacArthurian Christians would also take suggestions from other Christians about treating people with love and compassion and says things like, "You think every sermon should be about love, but a preacher needs to tell the truth about God's wrath."

As usual, they make a point that has nothing to do with the discussion. I have no problem with a pastor preaching fire and brimstone. I know some that do it almost every sermon. But they can do it without talking down to their congregation, without calling them names, and without judging them. If it takes using God's wrath and God's judgment to scare people into walking the narrow road, that's fine. We are supposed to fear these things.

But here's the point – it is GOD'S wrath. It is GOD's judgment.

Another thing MacArthurian Christians use to justify aggressive behavior is to claim that these are the end times.

These may well indeed be the end times but what does that

have to do with ignoring the teachings of Jesus?

In "Survival Strategy for Apostate Times, Part 1," MacArthur says:

We come now to the study of the Word of God and back to the epistle of Jude. And we find ourselves coming to verses 17 to 25 and there's definitely a turning point here.

This part of the epistle is addressed to us about how to survive in times of apostasy.

Let's look at those verses.

Jude 1:17-25

17But, dear friends, remember what the apostles of our Lord Jesus Christ foretold. 18They said to you, "In the last times there will be scoffers who will follow their own ungodly desires." 19These are the men who divide you, who follow mere natural instincts and do not have the Spirit.

20But you, dear friends, build yourselves up in your most holy faith and pray in the Holy Spirit. 21Keep yourselves in God's love as you wait for the mercy of our Lord Jesus Christ to bring you to eternal life.

22Be merciful to those who doubt; 23snatch others from the fire and save them; to others show mercy, mixed with fear—hating even the clothing stained by corrupted flesh.

Doxology

24To him who is able to keep you from falling and to present you before his glorious presence without fault and with great joy— 25to the only God our Savior be glory, majesty, power and authority, through Jesus Christ our Lord, before all ages, now and forevermore! Amen.
(NIV)

You will notice that nowhere in these verses does it instruct us to act differently in the end times than it does any other time. In fact, it says the opposite. "Keep yourselves in God's love as you wait for the mercy of our Lord Jesus Christ to bring you to eternal life. Be merciful to those who doubt; snatch others from the fire and save them; to others show mercy, mixed with fear."

Still in "Survival Strategy for Apostate Times, Part 1,' MacArthur says:

> *There has always been a core of the true believers. But always they have been earnestly contending for the once-for-all-delivered-to-the-saints faith. They've always been, we've always been engaged in a war. And that's why I've told you all along, if you look at verse 3 that Jude's epistle is a call to arms, appealing to us to contend earnestly for the faith which was once for all delivered to the saints.*

"A call to arms?" Everything with MacArthur seems to be

about conflict, battle, or war. But does the third verse of Jude direct us to take up arms?

If you read the entire book of Jude, you will see that he is warning Christians about certain men who have slipped in among them, godless men, who will try to test their faith and lead them astray. This is something every Christian must contend with.

So it's easy to understand that "contend" here means to be prepared spiritually, to maintain your faith during these trying times.

Using this verse to promote the idea that Christians are supposed to go on the attack or act in any way differently than how Jesus instructed seems odd. How do I know? Because I read verse two before verse three.

Everywhere in the New Testament where it talks about the end times or the tribulation, it talks about things that will happen, signs to look for, and how scoffers and evil people will act.

But nowhere does it give Christians a different set of rules on how to behave as Christians during this time. Nowhere! It only says you should be prepared by having your house in order. In other words, don't wait until you think the end is near to follow the teachings of Jesus, do them now because you don't know when that time will be.

Matthew 24:36
"No one knows about that day or hour, not even the angels in heaven, nor the Son, but only the Father."
(NIV)

Matthew 24:42-44
"Therefore keep watch, because you do not know on what day your Lord will come. 43But understand this: If the owner of the house had known at what time of night the thief was coming, he would have kept watch and would not have let his house be broken into. 44So you also must be ready, because the Son of Man will come at an hour when you do not expect him.
(NIV)

Chapter Seven: God's Actions Versus God's Teaching

I've noticed a pattern with MacArthur and MacArthurian Christians. They seem to be of the mind set that if Jesus or God did it, then they are allowed, even expected, to do it as well. MacArthur has written many articles about Jesus not being nice and he concentrates a lot of time on pointing out the aggressive stance Jesus took with certain people of the time.

In "The Jesus You Can't Ignore: An Interview with Phil Johnson and John MacArthur," he says:

> *Well you know, Phil, we've got all kinds of e-mail saying Jesus came to bring peace, why do you want to start a war? So I began to think to myself, what Jesus are these people talking about? After all, Jesus said "I came not to bring peace but a sword." That's pretty graphic and unmistakable language. He said, "If you're going to follow Me...it may come down to this, hate your father, hate your mother, hate your own life, take up your cross and follow Me." This is a discipleship call that could result in your martyrdom because the hostility against Me is so profound.*

It is because of teachings like this that I have tried many times to point out one very important thing to MacArthurian Christians - You are not Jesus.

It doesn't matter if Jesus used words like "fool" and "hypocrite." It doesn't matter if Jesus overturned the tables of the money changers in the temples. It doesn't matter if Jesus used a metaphor with the word "sword." You are not Him. You are only supposed to follow His words, not place yourself as high as He. No matter what actions Jesus took while he was on earth, never once did He say, "Do as I do, not as I say."

Even in the scripture from Matthew, chapter ten, used here by MacArthur where Jesus said, "Do not suppose that I have come to bring peace to the earth. I did not come to bring peace, but a sword," nowhere in this entire chapter does Jesus say to His disciples, or to us, that we are equal to Him and can mimic His actions.

He gives the opposite instructions throughout this entire chapter.

Matthew 10:14
"If anyone will not welcome you or listen to your words, shake the dust off your feet when you leave that home or town." (NIV)

Matthew 10:23
"When you are persecuted in one place, flee to another." (NIV)

Matthew 10:28
"Do not be afraid of those who kill the body but cannot kill the soul. Rather, be afraid of the One who can destroy both soul and body in hell." (NIV)

You can see that Jesus does not instruct them to take any kind of aggressive actions but instead tells them to "flee", "shake the dust off," and "Do not be afraid of those who kill the body..."

In "What DID Jesus Do?" MacArthur writes:

> **What did Jesus do? How did He deal with the false teachers, religious hypocrites, and theological miscreants of His time? Did He favor the approach of friendly dialogue and collegial disagreement, or did He in fact adopt a militant stance against every form of false religion?**

Yes, He took a militant stance in that He was aggressive but not a militant stance as in physical war. But unlike the bumper sticker, should the question really be "What would Jesus do?" or like MacArthur says, "What DID Jesus do?"

I think neither. I think the question should be - "What would Jesus have us do?" If you read through the Bible, you will find no verses where we are told that we are equal to God. You will find no verses where Jesus instructs us to ignore His message and to mimic His actions.

Should Christians use the actions of Jesus to ignore the teachings of Jesus?

Think about it. This was the very first trick Satan used on

man, making him believe that he could be equal to God.

Genesis 3:4-5
4"You will not surely die," the serpent said to the woman. 5 "For God knows that when you eat of it your eyes will be opened, and you will be like God, knowing good and evil." (NIV)

I guess the old saying is true, "if it ain't broke, don't fix it." Satan's first trick of making us think we can be equal to God might still be his best trick.

So anytime someone tells you that just because Jesus or God did something, then you're allowed to do it too, think about the original sin and what it was all about before concluding that you can substitute the actions of Jesus for the teachings of Jesus.

Chapter Eight: War

This is a tough call for most Christians. But all the aggressive and angry talk from MacArthurian Christians made me wonder about their stance on war. When asked, it didn't take long for them to come back with many verses from the Old Testament and from Revelation to justify their firm stance on war.

When asked to provide scripture from the New Testament to affirm their pro-war beliefs, one offered this:

> Ephesians 6::13-16
> 13Therefore put on the full armor of God, so that when the day of evil comes, you may be able to stand your ground, and after you have done everything, to stand. 14Stand firm then, with the belt of truth buckled around your waist, with the breastplate of righteousness in place, 15and with your feet fitted with the readiness that comes from the gospel of peace. 16In addition to all this, take up the shield of faith, with which you can extinguish all the flaming arrows of the evil one. (NIV)

Once again, I tried to point out that this was a metaphor. It's not talking about real armor and physical battle. If they could have just backed up one verse, this would have been clear.

> Ephesians 6::12
> For our struggle is not against flesh and blood... (NIV)

Clearly, putting on the "belt of truth," the "breastplate of righteousness," and "with the readiness that comes from the gospel of peace," is not talking about a nation going to war in a struggle against flesh and blood.

In "The Believer's Armor: God's Provision for Your Protection," MacArthur says:

> **The Christian life is a battle. It is warfare on a grand scale.**

Maybe it's words like this that make MacArthurian Christians so ready and willing to strike up conflict with others.

In "What Does the Bible Say About War? Is There Ever a Just Reason for it?" MacArthur says:

> **Through the centuries, three main viewpoints have emerged from within the church in response to the question of war:**
> **Some believe no war is justifiable (a position called pacifism). Others believe Christians must submit to their government and agree to fight in any war it engages in (a viewpoint known as activism). But the majority of Christians hold the view that believers may support or join in defensive wars against evil aggressors--a position known as the just war theory.**
>
> **We identify ourselves with the third approach--the just war theory.**

This is accurate. Most of my Christian friends who are not

followers of John MacArthur take this very stance. I've heard it said many times that they support the war if it's a just war.

But when we decide for ourselves what is just, it's amazing how it seems to emulate our patriotic values. So far, from what I've gathered from my own personal views and from Christians of all different denominations who support war, the just wars that we support seem to be the ones the USA participates in. It's incredible how we seem to have a monopoly on just wars.

Likewise, going by MacArthur's description above, he says we should support defensive wars against evil aggressors. But again, it creates a lot of room for personal judgment deciding what is "defensive" and who is "evil."

Clearly the hijackers who attacked us on 9/11 were "evil" but was invading Iraq, a country who had not attacked us, a "defensive" move? A lot of people try to make the case that it was, that these people hated us and it was just a matter of time before they attacked us.

I, myself, have made that claim in my attempt to make this war a "defensive" war and to make this war a "just" war. But if I stopped and thought about it, and I was completely honest with myself, I know in my heart that it is my patriotism that creates these thoughts and feelings and not the teachings of Jesus.

But to even question the war in Iraq like a lot of Christians felt the need to do, brought about more scorn and attacks from the MacArthurian Christians.

Again, In "What Does the Bible Say About War? Is There Ever a Just Reason for it?" MacArthur says:

> **Because life is precious, God decreed its preservation and protection by calling for the punishment of anyone who murders a bearer of His image. He issued this command when Noah left the ark to begin a fresh start on dry land:**
> **Surely I will require your lifeblood; from every beast I will require it. And from every man, from every man's brother I will require the life of man. Whoever sheds man's blood, by man his blood shall be shed, for in the image of God He made man. (Genesis 9:5-6)**

This is talking about one person, not nations going to war. And we already established that "an eye for an eye" was a rule of the Old Testament and a rule that Jesus specifically amended. It amazes me that MacArthur uses "eye for an eye" to justify so many things.

Again, In "What Does the Bible Say About War? Is There Ever a Just Reason for it?" MacArthur says:

> **In the New Testament, the apostle Paul declares that God empowers governments to punish those who do evil. Civil officials are told to bear the sword as avengers and execute wrath on those who practice wickedness:**

78

Every person is to be in subjection to the governing authorities. For there is no authority except from God, and those which exist are established by God. Therefore whoever resists authority has opposed the ordinance of God; and they who have opposed will receive condemnation upon themselves. For rulers are not a cause of fear for good behavior, but for evil. Do you want to have no fear of authority? Do what is good and you will have praise from the same; for it is a minister of God to you for good. But if you do what is evil, be afraid; for it does not bear the sword for nothing; for it is a minister of God, an avenger who brings wrath on the one who practices evil. Therefore it is necessary to be in subjection, not only because of wrath, but also for conscience' sake. For because of this you also pay taxes, for rulers are servants of God, devoting themselves to this very thing. Render to all what is due them: tax to whom tax is due; custom to whom custom; fear to whom fear; honor to whom honor. (Romans 13:1-7)

First Peter 2:13-14 is in agreement--God ordained government to ensure order in society by punishing evildoers:
Submit yourselves for the Lord's sake to every human institution, whether to a king as the one in authority, or to governors as sent by him for the punishment of evildoers and the praise of those who do right.

Just like MacArthur seems to use the penal system to try to justify personal judgment, he seems to use it again here to justify war. But none of this is talking about nations going to war; it's talking about breaking criminal laws and being punished accordingly.

To further justify war, MacArthurian Christians use Luke 22:36

Luke 22:36
He said to them, "But now if you have a purse, take it, and also a bag; and if you don't have a sword, sell your cloak and buy one."
(NIV)

Jesus did instruct his disciples to buy a sword, but was it for protection or aggression. That is answered in Luke 22:49-51

Luke 22:40-51
49When Jesus' followers saw what was going to happen, they said, "Lord, should we strike with our swords?" 50And one of them struck the servant of the high priest, cutting off his right ear.
51But Jesus answered, "No more of this!" And he touched the man's ear and healed him.
(NIV)

Time and time again, MacArthur and MacArthurian Christians seem to search for bits and pieces of scripture to justify their beliefs when a lot of times the very next verse(s) or the previous verse(s) go against what they're claiming.

Jesus was not promoting aggression or war here. I think he knew that without a sword, one of his disciples might be killed trying to protect him and he still had work for them to do. But as soon as one of his followers struck out in an aggressive mode, he put a stop to it and healed the enemy.

Is it accurate to say that Jesus was about war or that he wanted us to be? I can find no place in the teaching of Jesus where he did endorse war.

Do you know that the word "war" is mentioned only 14 times in the New Testament and half of those are in Revelation speaking about the prophecy, the war the Heaven, etc.

Here are the seven other places.

Matthew 24:6
You will hear of wars and rumors of wars, but see to it that you are not alarmed. Such things must happen, but the end is still to come.
(NIV

Mark 13:7
When you hear of wars and rumors of wars, do not be alarmed. Such things must happen, but the end is still to come.
(NIV)

Luke 14:31
"Or suppose a king is about to go to war against another king. Will he not first sit down and consider whether he is able with

ten thousand men to oppose the one coming against him with twenty thousand?
(NIV)

Luke 21:9
When you hear of wars and revolutions, do not be frightened. These things must happen first, but the end will not come right away.
(NIV)

Romans 7:23
but I see another law at work in the members of my body, waging war against the law of my mind and making me a prisoner of the law of sin at work within my members.
(NIV)

Corinthians 10:3
For though we live in the world, we do not wage war as the world does
(NIV)

1 Peter 2:11
Dear friends, I urge you, as aliens and strangers in the world, to abstain from sinful desires, which war against your soul.
(NIV)

Three of these are talking about rumors of wars. Two are talking about war against your mind or soul. One is using a metaphor about a king making sure he can achieve victory before going to war so he's telling the disciples that they must make sure they can make all the sacrifices needed to be a disciple before following him.

The only one of the 14 that applies to Christians and war is Corinthians 10:3 where it says that Christians "do not wage war."

Incidentally, "war" is mentioned over 2000 times on John MacArthur's web site.

And for the record, in the new Testament, the word "love" is mentioned 261 times. "Peace" is mentioned 109 times, and forms of the word "forgive" are mentioned 64 times, dependant upon what version you're reading.

Another conflict is how do you support war and embrace "love your enemy?" Can those things coexist? I know you can spank a child with love, but can you shot bullets, fire missiles and drop bombs with love?

I searched MacArthur's writings and found numerous articles and sermons on "love your enemy." Amazingly, unlike "turn the other cheek," and "judge not," MacArthur seems to embrace this concept fully. It was surprising for a man who seems to also embrace war so openly.

In an interview with Larry King just 18 days after the terrorist attacks on the World Trade Center, King asked MacArthur if he forgives the attackers.

MacArthur replies:

> *Oh, absolutely, and I can do that because I need forgiveness. But God is on another level. God, who is perfectly holy, will bring about a holy justice in the case of those individuals.*

I think that's the right answer but how do you go from that answer to supporting going to war with them?

In "Christ's Triumphant Death," MacArthur says:

> *It wasn't the terrorists who wreaked the real havoc on the people who died in the tower and in the Pentagon. All the terrorist's could do was kill their body. It was God who dispatched their eternal souls into everlasting punishment that wreaked the real havoc*

I had to read this several times because I just could not believe what MacArthur seemed to be saying here. Is he really saying that every American who died in the attacks of 9/11, God "dispatched their eternal souls to everlasting punishment?"

That's how it reads. If so, not only does this sicken me, but it's very judgmental and the rudest comment I've ever read concerning the victims of that day.

84

I'm quite certain that there were a lot of Christians who were killed that day and who will have eternal life with our Lord.

There's nothing wrong with being confused with the question of war being right or wrong. These are things we should talk about. Sometimes it's hard to see clearly around our personal views, our patriotic views, and our own human nature to know what the stance of a Christian should be.

But I have read the Bible many times and nowhere in the New Testament do I find where Jesus instructed us to wage war or even support war.

I believe that if we knew about the plans of the terrorists ahead of time, Jesus would have wanted us to take measures to prevent the loss of innocent life. I believe he would want us to take defensive measures to try to make sure the handful of people who planned this could not take more innocent life.

But regardless of how I feel or all of my friends feel about the war in Iraq, knowing the Bible like I do, I can't believe that Jesus is smiling upon that venture.

Chapter Nine: The Elect

We have touched upon the "Elect" or the "saints" many times so now let's try to figure out who this is referring to.

According to MacArthur, the Elect or the saints are everyone who will be saved.

In "God's Grace Displayed for His Glory," MacArthur says:

There are, as my grandfather used to say, only two kinds of people, the saints and the aints.

What a vulgar and crude expression. But this sums up the mentality of every MacArthurian Christian that I've ever met. We're special. We got it and you don't and there's nothing you can do to get it.

Here are some of the verses in the Bible tat MacArthur uses to affirm his belief.

Ephesians 1:4-5
According as he hath chosen us in him before the foundation of the world, that we should be holy and without blame before him in love:
5Having predestinated us unto the adoption of children by Jesus Christ to himself, according to the good pleasure of his will,   (KJB)

1 Corinthians 6:2
Do ye not know that the saints shall judge the world? and if the world shall be judged by you, are ye unworthy to judge the smallest matters?
(KJB)

2 Thessalonians 2:13
But we are bound to give thanks alway to God for you, brethren beloved of the Lord, because God hath from the beginning chosen you to salvation through sanctification of the Spirit and belief of the truth:
(KJB)

"Hath Chosen us..."
"Having predestined us..."
"The saints shall judge the world…"
"God hath from the beginning chosen you…"

This can be pretty convincing language and it might be easy to pat yourself on the back thinking you're a shoe-in to Heaven. I mean, that's got to be better than even winning the lottery.

There's only one problem with taking verses like these and claiming that this is meaning you, or anyone else, or especially meaning everyone who will have everlasting life. The problem is, these were all letters directed to specific groups of people. Paul wrote the letter to the people of the church in Corinth, he wrote the letter to the people of the church in Ephesus, and

Paul and Timothy wrote the letter to the people of the church of Thessalonica.

As pointed out earlier, these were churches and Christians who preached the gospel of Jesus in a time when it was very dangerous to do so. It's not hard to believe that these Christians would make up part of the Elect.

But to take these letters that were directed at a specific group of people and claim that Paul was instead talking about you, is silly at best. It's like finding another student's test paper and it having an A plus grade and claiming the grade was for you.

But again, nowhere in the New Testament does Jesus say that every person saved was predestined.

Another argument MacArthurian Christians make is that God is all knowing so he would know who was saved and therefore it has to be predestined.

But I contend that knowing what decision a person will make does not take away the free will for them to make that decision. If you put a child in a room and tell him there are two gifts to choose from and he can pick whichever he wants, and one gift is a new bike and one gift is a bucket of broken glass, do you know which gift he will choose? Of course, but it doesn't mean he didn't have free will to make the choice.

The whole belief that some people were just lucky and nothing makes a difference goes against the key message of the Bible. There are so many verses in the Bible that talks about Jesus trying to save people and of sending out his disciples to try to save people.

Paul did the same.

1 Corinthians 9:19-23
19Though I am free and belong to no man, I make myself a slave to everyone, to win as many as possible. 20To the Jews I became like a Jew, to win the Jews. To those under the law I became like one under the law (though I myself am not under the law), so as to win those under the law. 21To those not having the law I became like one not having the law (though I am not free from God's law but am under Christ's law), so as to win those not having the law. 22To the weak I became weak, to win the weak. I have become all things to all men so that by all possible means I might save some. 23I do all this for the sake of the gospel, that I may share in its blessings. (NIV)

Look at what all Paul was willing to do just to try to save as many as he could.

And we all remember the rich man asking Jesus how to inherit eternal life. Why wouldn't Jesus just tell him that it was decided long ago? But he didn't.

Mark 10:17-21

17As Jesus started on his way, a man ran up to him and fell on his knees before him. "Good teacher," he asked, "what must I do to inherit eternal life?"

18"Why do you call me good?" Jesus answered. "No one is good—except God alone. 19You know the commandments: 'Do not murder, do not commit adultery, do not steal, do not give false testimony, do not defraud, honor your father and mother.'"

20"Teacher," he declared, "all these I have kept since I was a boy."

21Jesus looked at him and loved him. "One thing you lack," he said. "Go, sell everything you have and give to the poor, and you will have treasure in heaven. Then come, follow me." (NIV)

Here are other verses to reinforce this.

John 3:3:
"...no one can see the kingdom of God unless he is born again." (NIV)

John 3:15:
"...everyone who believes in him [Jesus] may have eternal life." (NIV)

John 3:18:
"...whoever does not believe stands condemned already because he has not believed in the name of God's one and only Son.
(NIV)

John 14:6:
"Jesus answered: 'No one comes to the Father except through me'"
(NIV)

Romans 10:9:
"Everyone who calls on the name of the Lord will be saved"
(NIV)

The whole premise that the Elect makes up everyone saved and nothing can change that goes against all these verses. It also goes against the very reason Jesus came to earth.

Nothing explains that better than Matthew 9:10-13

Matthew 89:10-13
10While Jesus was having dinner at Matthew's house, many tax collectors and "sinners" came and ate with him and his disciples. 11When the Pharisees saw this, they asked his disciples, "Why does your teacher eat with tax collectors and 'sinners'?"
12On hearing this, Jesus said, "It is not the healthy who need

a doctor, but the sick. 13But go and learn what this means: 'I desire mercy, not sacrifice.' For I have not come to call the righteous, but sinners."
(NIV)

Where MacArthur took the verse where Jesus used a metaphor about coming not to bring peace but to bring a sword, to justify an aggressive Christian image, he said, "So I began to think to myself, what Jesus are these people talking about?"

I think you're both talking about the same Jesus, some just pay more attention to his lessons and some more to his actions. I think you're both wrong. I don't think Jesus came to bring peace and I certainly don't think he came to bring war. So why did Jesus come?

Matthew 18:12-14
12"What do you think? If a man owns a hundred sheep, and one of them wanders away, will he not leave the ninety-nine on the hills and go to look for the one that wandered off? 13And if he finds it, I tell you the truth, he is happier about that one sheep than about the ninety-nine that did not wander off. 14In the same way your Father in heaven is not willing that any of these little ones should be lost.
(NIV)

Luke 9:56
For the Son of man is not come to destroy men's lives, but to

save them.
(KJV)

John 3:17
For God did not send his Son into the world to condemn the world, but to save the world through him.
(NIV)

1 Timothy 1:15
Here is a trustworthy saying that deserves full acceptance: Christ Jesus came into the world to save sinners—of whom I am the worst.
(NIV)

2 Peter 3:9
The Lord is not slow in keeping his promise, as some understand slowness. He is patient with you, not wanting anyone to perish, but everyone to come to repentance.
(NIV)

You cannot read these simple lessons and believe that we do not have a choice to do God's will and that everyone, even the tax collectors and sinners, have the same chance for salvation as everyone else.

And remember the verses earlier that MacArthur tried to use as evidence we are supposed to act more aggressively during the end times?

Jude 1:17-25

17But, dear friends, remember what the apostles of our Lord Jesus Christ foretold. 18They said to you, "In the last times there will be scoffers who will follow their own ungodly desires." 19These are the men who divide you, who follow mere natural instincts and do not have the Spirit.

20But you, dear friends, build yourselves up in your most holy faith and pray in the Holy Spirit. 21Keep yourselves in God's love as you wait for the mercy of our Lord Jesus Christ to bring you to eternal life.

22Be merciful to those who doubt; 23snatch others from the fire and save them; to others show mercy, mixed with fear— hating even the clothing stained by corrupted flesh.

(NIV)

You'll notice that even here, during the worst times man will ever go through, we are still supposed to try and save as many as we can. "Snatch others from the fire and save them."

How can we, mere mortals, be able to save anyone from the fire if God made that decision long ago?

So who are the Elect? I think the Bible is very clear on who they are and what their role will be.

Revelation 20:4

I saw thrones on which were seated those who had been given authority to judge. And I saw the souls of those who had been

beheaded because of their testimony for Jesus and because of the word of God. They had not worshiped the beast or his image and had not received his mark on their foreheads or their hands. They came to life and reigned with Christ a thousand years.
(NIV)

If everyone saved makes up the Elect, then who are they judging and why are they judging them? It explains that. After the 1000 years, here's what happens.

Revelation 20:12-15
12And I saw the dead, great and small, standing before the throne, and books were opened. Another book was opened, which is the book of life. The dead were judged according to what they had done as recorded in the books. 13The sea gave up the dead that were in it, and death and Hades gave up the dead that were in them, and each person was judged according to what he had done. 14Then death and Hades were thrown into the lake of fire. The lake of fire is the second death. 15If anyone's name was not found written in the book of life, he was thrown into the lake of fire.
(NIV)

So it clearly states here that the Elect will be judging everyone else. And of those, some people's names will be found written in the book of life and they will have everlasting life.

But if MacArthur's theory was correct, all of the saved would be up there with the ones judging. You can see that is not the case.

So if the Elect is not made up of everyone saved, then who are they?

Some believe that the 144,000 is referring to the Elect. There are several possible theories, however, and I cannot honestly say which is correct.

But with all the verses in the Bible which talk about Jesus coming to this world to save sinners or anyone who would come to repentance, it makes MacArthur's theory sound ridiculous to me.

When you look at all Paul did to save as many souls as he could, it makes MacArthur's theory sound ridiculous to me.

When you look at our instructions for during the end times, when things will be very bleak, even then we are instructed to save as many as we can. When you consider this, it makes MacArthur's theory sound ridiculous to me.

All you have to do is read the Bible and understand the difference of when Jesus is giving you instructions and when someone is writing a letter to a specific group of people. And more importantly, know better than to look for loopholes to try and change the simple instructions.

If we can do that, we will know that there are not two groups called "the saints and the aints." We will know that there are only God's children, those who are saved and those we need to try to save.

Now I know why MacArthurian Christians, when presented with beliefs that were at odds with their own, only went on the attack. I couldn't understand it before. Why, I wondered, if they truly believed someone had faulty information and was at risk of not being saved, why wouldn't they try to save them? Now it makes sense. Salvation belongs to the Elect, to lucky people like them, and there's nothing anyone can do to change that.

It is your choice whether you want to take the words from letters that Paul and Timothy wrote to specific groups of people, and claim that they were meaning you, or do you want to follow the teaching of Jesus and know that salvation is yours but you have to earn it.

Chapter Ten: Do We Change the Message?

I'll begin this chapter with a very powerful message from John MacArthur.

From "A Portrait of False Teachers, Part 1," he says:

> *Is there a more serious crime than falsifying the truth of the Word of God? Is there anything worse than lying about God, Christ, the Holy Spirit or the meaning of Scripture? Is there a severer crime than teaching the devil's lies as if they were God's truth? Is there anything more infuriating to God than misrepresentation of His Word? Is there a worse hypocrisy than saying you speak for God to the salvation of souls when in reality you speak for Satan to the damnation of souls? Can there be a more heinous deception than being a false teacher in the church?*

These are all great questions.

> Proverbs 30:5-6
> 5 "Every word of God is flawless;
>   he is a shield to those who take refuge in him.
> 6 Do not add to his words,
>   or he will rebuke you and prove you a liar.
> (NIV)

I think we all know we should never change or add to the Word of God, which of course includes the teachings of

Jesus. The problem is, it becomes a finger pointing fiasco with everyone of different views claiming it is the other who does that. That's why I say to read the Bible by yourself. Try to read it with no preconceived ideas about what or who you want to believe.

I know the words of Jesus are, "If someone strikes you on the right cheek, turn to him the other also." I know that He is not using a metaphor here since this is in a succession of six specific rules He is revising during the Sermon on the Mount and He doesn't use a metaphor in any of them. So I believe that He used these specific for a reason.

So when I discuss this verse, these are the exact words I use because I don't want to change them.

But is that not what happens when you literally substitute phrases like getting walked all over, someone stealing all you own, or getting mugged at night while you're a vulnerable position and laying down? Is it not changing the words to say Jesus was instead meaning getting flogged, humiliated, thrown out of the church, or receiving 39 lashes?

Is it not changing His words to say the words "judge not" does not apply to us but to the Pharisees and scribes?

Is it not changing words to take the letter from Paul where he tells the people of the church of Corinth that they will judge the world at the end times and say that means all Christians and it means now? Is it not changing the words to take the word "discern" and give it the same meaning as the word "judging?"

Is it not changing the words to take some parts of the Old Testament (old agreement), besides the moral lessons like the Ten Commandments, and claim they still apply today?

Is it not changing the words to say we can act like Jesus acted or do the things Jesus did when the Bible doesn't instruct us to do so?

Is it not changing the words to say that Jesus was about war? If we choose to ignore phrases like "Blessed are the meek", "Blessed are the merciful", "Blessed are the peacemakers", "Rejoice and be glad", "love your enemy," and many other verses like these and take a few other verses which include metaphors to make the case that Jesus promotes war or instructs us to do so, is that not changing the words?

We know all too well that there are some in the Islam faith that ignore the parts of the Quran about peace, love, and compassion and concentrate on the parts about hate, aggression, judgment and war. But is it the best way for Christians to deal with Islam, to try to make Christianity more like it?

When I read the teachings of John MacArthur about waging

war and us being at war or any reference to the actions of Jesus being militant, etc., I sometimes have trouble telling the difference in MacArthur's teachings and the beliefs of Islamic extremist.

Some people believe that the Bible is so complicated that you need someone to translate it for you. I think that's an absurd notion. I think the teachings of Jesus are easy to understand. Like MacArthur said, if you want to know where you stand as a Christian, read the Sermon on the Mount.

But if you think you need an interpreter to decipher the Bible for you, you might want to pay close attention to the interpretations.

If that interpreter explains that "judge not" is instructing you to judge, you might want to question that.

If that interpreter explains that "turn the other cheek" is talking about receiving 39 lashes and doesn't apply to you, you might want to question that.

If that interpreter explains that you are supposed to pick-and-choose whichever rules from the Old Testament you want, you might want to question that.

If that interpreter explains that the message of Jesus was an all out attack and that Jesus promotes war over peace, you might want to question that.

If that interpreter explains that Jesus is instructing you to act with anger and aggression, you might want to question that.

If that interpreter explains that you are one of the lucky ones that was predestined to be saved so you don't have to worry about your deeds, you might want to question that.

If that interpreter explains that you are equal to God and Jesus and can do whatever they did, I would seriously consider getting a new interpreter.

Read the Bible and its meaning will be clear to you. The Old Testament is a great study guide to understand the past. It explains the creation of the world and of man and gives us examples of God's love and God's wrath. Revelation is a great book to understand the future. It explains the second coming, the tribulation, and judgment.

Between the Old Testament and Revelation, you will find the teachings and lessons for all Christians. Read it carefully and you will find no verses where Christians are ever instructed to do anything negative. I've had MacArthurian Christians argue that it is not clear what actions are negative and which are positive but that's not true. We all have a clear understanding of positive and negative just as we all have a clear understanding of right and wrong.

But here are some examples. Love is positive; hate is negative. Accepting is positive; judging is negative. Forgiveness is positive; revenge is negative. Turning the other cheek is positive; fighting is negative. Rejoice and be glad is positive; anger and aggression are negative. Peace is positive; war is negative.

The rules set out over 2000 years ago still apply today as they did then and as they will right up until the very end. There is no room for evolution when it comes to the Word of God. It is never changing. The instructions are clear. They are not easy but they are clear. And nothing, including the end times or terrorists attacks can change that.

In the end, your decisions are all up to you. And that is the gift that God bestowed upon us - free will. It is also our greatest curse.

I'll end this book with one last quote from MacArthur.

From "The State of the Church, Part 2."

By the way, just to tell you what that means in Matthew 7, a wolf in sheep's clothing is a false prophet. Sheep's clothing is wool. Prophets wore wool. He is saying somebody might come dressed like a prophet but they're really a destructive wolf come to rip and tear.

***

God Bless

www.ingramcontent.com/pod-product-compliance
Lightning Source LLC
Chambersburg PA
CBHW021206020426
42331CB00003B/230